THE 12 MOST INFLUENTIAL
INVENTIONS OF ALL TIME

by Emily Rose Oachs

12
STORY
LIBRARY

www.12StoryLibrary.com

12-Story Library is an imprint of Bookstaves.

Photographs ©: Paul Sakuma/AP Images, cover, 1; North Wind Picture Archives, 4, 8, 10, 11, 14, 29; Geoffrey Holman/iStockphoto, 5; Benson HE/Shutterstock Images, 6; Sarah Bossert/iStockphoto, 7; Adam Szuly/iStockphoto, 9; Sirikornt/iStockphoto, 12; Hein Nouwens/Shutterstock Images, 13; sumire8/Shutterstock Images, 17; Mondadori Portfolio/Getty Images, 16; chuyuss/Shutterstock Images, 18, 28; Library of Congress, 19; AP Images, 20, 22; Scanrail1/Shutterstock Images, 21; Olha Rohulya/Shutterstock Images, 23; Eva Katalin Kondoros/iStockphoto, 25; Rawpixel.com/Shutterstock Images, 26; Zeynep Demir/Shutterstock Images, 27

Library of Congress Cataloging-in-Publication Data
Names: Oachs, Emily Rose, author.
Title: The 12 most influential inventions of all time / by Emily Rose Oachs.
Other titles: Twelve most influential inventions of all time
Description: Mankato, MN : 12 Story Library, 2017. | Series: The most
   influential | Includes bibliographical references and index. | Audience:
   Grades 4 to 6.
Identifiers: LCCN 2016047118 (print) | LCCN 2016048180 (ebook) | ISBN
   9781632354099 (hardcover : alk. paper) | ISBN 9781632354808 (pbk. : alk.
   paper) | ISBN 9781621435327 (hosted e-book)
Subjects: LCSH: Inventions--Juvenile literature.
Classification: LCC T48 .022 2017 (print) | LCC T48 (ebook) | DDC 600--dc23
LC record available at https://lccn.loc.gov/2016047118

Printed in the United States of America
July 2018

Access free, up-to-date content on this topic plus a full digital version of this book. Scan the QR code on page 31 or use your school's login at 12StoryLibrary.com.

Table of Contents

The Wheel Makes Life Easier

The wheel was a key ancient invention. It is a valuable technology that people still use today. Historians think people in modern Turkey, Iraq, and Iran invented the wheel around 3500 BCE. At first, wheels were used to make pottery. People placed clay on a spinning wheel to make bowls, cups, and pots.

BEFORE THE WHEEL

Many people consider the wheel to be one of the first inventions. However, other long-lasting inventions came first. Before the wheel, humans had already invented sewing needles, sailboats, and rope. Musical instruments such as harps and flutes also came earlier.

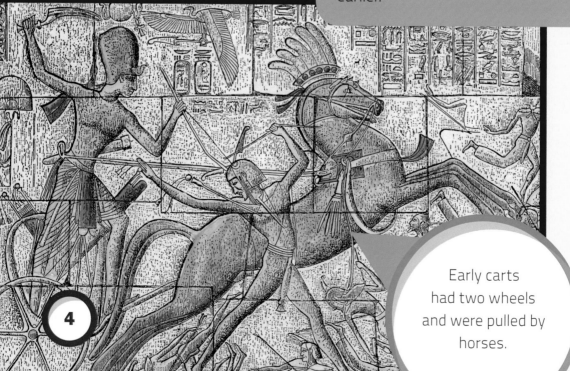

Early carts had two wheels and were pulled by horses.

THINK ABOUT IT

How has the wheel changed since it was first invented? How has it stayed the same? What are new uses for the wheel? Research online to find out more.

500

Estimated number of years between the wheel's invention and its use in transportation.

- Using the wheel for transportation started around 3000 BCE.
- With the wheel, humans could haul heavy loads over land.
- Other inventions use the wheel, such as cars, waterwheels, and gears.

Wheels improved transportation, too. Around 3000 BCE, people began building carts and wagons with wheels. Animals pulled the loaded wagons and carts over land. This made it easier to haul heavy items over long distances. In particular, it helped farmers carry food and crops into cities.

Later, people made other inventions using the wheel. These include waterwheels, pulleys, and gears. Today, wheels are a common feature in everyday life. Without the wheel, the world would not have cars, wheelbarrows, bicycles, or Ferris wheels.

People made the first wheels out of wood or stone.

Gunpowder Makes War Deadlier

In the 800s, Chinese alchemists were searching for a recipe for immortality. They experimented with many different ingredients to try to create it. One day, an alchemist mixed saltpeter, sulfur, and charcoal. The result was a fast-burning powder. The alchemists had found gunpowder instead of immortality!

At first, the Chinese only made fireworks with the gunpowder. Soon, they began to use gunpowder to create weapons. They needed strong weapons to fight off northern attackers. They launched arrows that held flaming packages of gunpowder. They also created early versions of cannons, grenades, rockets, and guns.

Gradually, gunpowder's recipe spread west. Gunpowder reached the Middle East and Europe by the mid-1300s. It forever changed war. Gunpowder became a destructive element in weapons. New gunpowder-based weapons appeared, such as pistols and muskets.

In addition to their use as weapons, early Chinese rockets were also used to launch fireworks for celebrations.

Early muskets powered by gunpowder produced tremendous amounts of smoke when fired.

Each was more powerful than the last.

Gunpowder changed how people fought wars. Early weapons, such as swords, had depended on a soldier's strength and skill. With gunpowder, anyone could cause damage with a powerful weapon. It was also harder to defend against these new weapons. Soldiers, armies, and wars became much more deadly.

285.3 million

Pounds (129.4 million kg) of fireworks used in the United States on July 4, 2016.

- Chinese alchemists first created gunpowder in the 800s.
- Gunpowder spread from China to the Middle East and Europe by the 1300s.
- Gunpowder made war deadlier than ever before.

The Printing Press Spreads Knowledge

Before the printing press, many books were written out by hand. Some books were also printed using wooden blocks. To do this, a printer carved the words for each page from a piece of wood. Both ways of making books were slow. They were also costly. Only rich people could afford books. As a result, only rich people had access to written knowledge.

That changed in the 1440s. At that time, Johannes Gutenberg invented the printing press. Gutenberg's press was different from earlier ones. It used moveable type. He had many metal casts of each letter and punctuation

Johannes Gutenberg examines a printed page as it comes off the press.

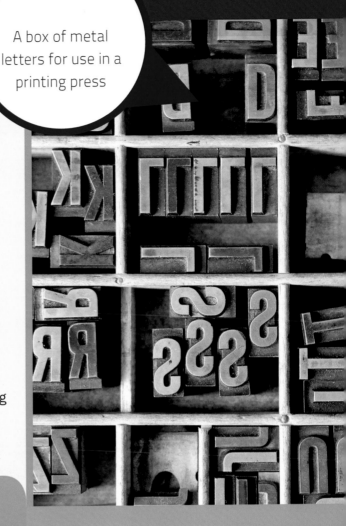

A box of metal letters for use in a printing press

mark. He arranged them one at a time to form sentences. Then, he could reuse and rearrange those letters for the next page.

Gutenberg's printing press allowed him to easily print thousands of book pages a day. It made books less expensive. More people could afford to buy books, and more people learned to read. The increase in books spread ideas and information to more people. Gutenberg's printing press brought knowledge to the masses.

3,600
Number of pages one of Gutenberg's printing presses could print in a day.

- The Gutenberg printing press made books faster and cheaper to produce.
- Books were no longer only for wealthy people.
- Books, knowledge, and ideas spread more quickly after the invention of the printing press.

BOOK BOOM

The number of books in Europe exploded after the invention of the printing press. Only approximately 30,000 books were in all of Europe in 1440. Within 50 years, there were as many as 12 million books in Europe. By 1600, more than 200 million books were on the continent.

4

The Steam Engine Creates New Power

For thousands of years, humans and animals provided most of the world's power. People also relied on power from wind and water. These power sources had problems. People and animals grew tired. Waterpower required being near a body of water. Wind power depended on the weather.

That all changed with Englishman Thomas Savery's invention. In 1698,

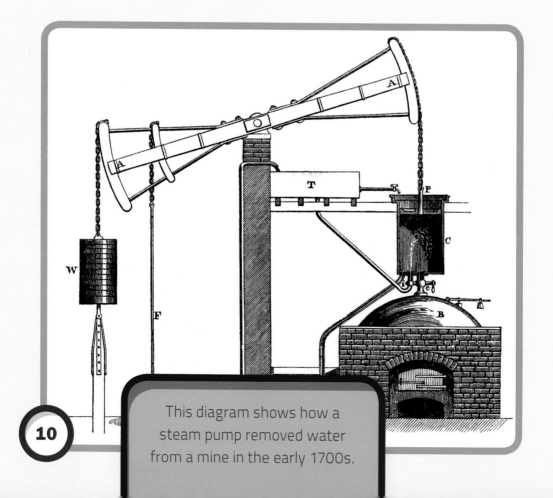

This diagram shows how a steam pump removed water from a mine in the early 1700s.

Militaries relied on steamships, such as the SS *Iowa*.

he patented the first steam engine. It used heat and steam to create energy. Savery used it to pump water from deep mines. The steam engine brought a new kind of power to the world. It was reliable and could be used anywhere.

Other inventors kept improving Savery's design. By the 1760s, the steam engine had new uses. Factories and mills used them to power machines. They produced goods faster and more cheaply than ever before. The new factories and mills created many jobs, too. Thousands of people moved from the country to cities with factories.

The steam engine also changed transportation. In 1804, the first steam train made its way down a set of tracks in Wales. Three years later, the first successful steamship made a voyage. Steam trains and steamships allowed people to travel long distances in less time than ever before.

2,000
Number of steam engines built in England by 1800.

- Thomas Savery patented the first steam engine in 1698.
- The steam engine was a new source of energy.
- It powered factories, mills, and new types of transportation.

Indoor Plumbing Improves Health

Less disease and better access to clean water came with indoor plumbing. Indoor plumbing started to be installed in New York City in the 1840s. Engineers built an aqueduct that carried water into the city. This water was stored in large reservoirs. Underground pipes then brought this water into buildings and homes.

Indoor plumbing was slow to catch on. It was very expensive to install. At first, only the wealthy could afford it. Few families had indoor plumbing in the 1860s. But by 1940, about half of Americans had running water and toilets. Today, most American homes have indoor plumbing.

Indoor plumbing has many benefits. Previously, people had to fetch water from a stream, river, or well each

> Indoor plumbing keeps people clean, safe, and comfortable.

1.6 gallons

Average amount of water one toilet flush uses.

- Indoor plumbing first came to New York City in the 1840s.
- It helped prevent the spread of deadly diseases such as cholera and yellow fever.
- According to the US Census Bureau, 1.6 million Americans live without indoor plumbing today.

day. Then they had to carry it home. But indoor plumbing provided people with clean water much faster. They simply had to turn a faucet.

Americans also began to install toilets in their homes. Before toilets, people used outhouses and chamber pots. Human waste was often dumped into rivers and streams, polluting the water. The polluted water led to deadly outbreaks of diseases, such as yellow fever, cholera, and typhoid. But indoor plumbing connected toilets to underground sewers. Sewers carried waste away safely. It greatly reduced diseases spread through human waste.

Early toilets had tanks mounted on the wall. To flush, a person pulled a chain.

HISTORY OF TOILET PAPER

The Chinese first invented toilet paper in the 800s. But in most places, people did not use it. Instead, they wiped with what they could find. They used rope, book pages, sponges, and even corncobs! Indoor plumbing brought the return of toilet paper. In 1890, the Scott brothers made the first successful toilet paper rolls.

The Telephone Speeds Communication

In 1876, Alexander Graham Bell found a way to send sound over wires. Bell's first words over the telephone were to his assistant. He said, "Mr. Watson, come here; I want you." Bell's telephone changed how

Alexander Graham Bell places the first long-distance call between New York and Chicago.

11 million

Number of telephones in the United States within 40 years of its invention.

- Alexander Graham Bell invented the telephone in 1876.
- Long-distance calls became possible in 1892.
- The telephone allowed people to speak across great distances.

ANSWERING THE PHONE

Two rival telephone companies started after the telephone's invention. Alexander Graham Bell founded the American Bell Telephone Company in 1880. The inventor Thomas Edison worked for Western Union. Bell and Edison had different opinions of how people should answer the phone. Edison believed people should say "Hello." Bell argued that the best way to answer was "Hoy, hoy!"

people communicate. It allowed people to speak easily to others who were far away.

Bell's telephone became popular quickly. Telephone poles went up around the country. Thousands of people had the devices installed in their homes.

Early telephones had no dials or buttons. To make a call, a person lifted the receiver and talked to an operator. The operator connected the caller with the person he or she wanted to reach. Then in 1891, a new invention allowed a caller to dial a person directly. Earlier callers could only place calls in their local area. Later, amplifiers and copper telephone wires allowed people to place calls over long distances.

Before telephones, people could only connect over long distances using telegraphs and letters. The telephone made communication faster, cheaper, and more convenient. People could chat with distant friends and family from their own homes. The telephone helped the world become more connected.

15

The Lightbulb Lights the World

For years, people had used gas and oil lamps to light the night. These lamps were smoky and unsafe. Many people experimented with using electricity as a new way to get light. In 1880, Thomas Edison patented his lightbulb design. The lightbulb's special filament allowed it to burn longer than other lightbulbs. It was also cheaper.

Soon, electric lightbulbs lit up the night. They let people see easily and safely long after sunset. All they had to do was flip a switch. Lightbulbs also changed daily schedules. People no longer had to plan their days around daylight. They could do activities that required light even after the sun went down.

Many factories also took advantage of the lightbulb. Its light allowed workers to labor all night long. Some factories started having workers do overnight shifts. This helped factories

Thomas Edison holds a lightbulb he designed.

600

Number of hours one of Edison's lightbulbs lasted in 1880.

- Thomas Edison patented the first successful light bulb in 1880.
- Electric lighting enabled people to work and socialize later into the evening.
- Edison brought electricity into factories and people's homes.

produce more goods.

Lightbulbs have improved over the years. New LED lightbulbs are brighter and last longer than earlier bulbs. They also use less energy. In 2012 alone, US homes and businesses used more than 49 million LED bulbs.

Today, buyers can choose from incandescent (top), compact fluorescent (middle), and LED (bottom) lightbulbs.

The Automobile Makes Travel Easier

The automobile changed transportation in a massive way. But early versions of the automobile were slow and bulky. The first modern automobile came in 1886. The Benz Motor Car No. 1 had two seats and three wheels. It was built by Karl Benz. It was the first car powered by gasoline.

By the early 1900s, many other carmakers were at work. Among them was Ford Motor Company. Henry Ford found a way to build cars cheaply and quickly. The cars were called the Model T. Soon, car prices began to fall. Lower prices meant more people could afford cars.

Automobiles quickly became the most common type of

Today, the world has more than 1 billion cars in it.

THINK ABOUT IT

The automobile depends on many different parts to run. What other inventions had to come before the automobile? When and by whom were those invented? Read and research online to learn about those car parts.

50

Percent of automobiles on the road in 1920 that were Model T Fords.

- Karl Benz patented his design for the first modern automobile in 1886.
- Cars quickly became popular and available to everyday people.
- Automobiles changed where people lived and how they got around.

transportation. They allowed people to travel more freely. People could work in the city but live outside it. As a result, people started to move out of cities and into suburbs.

The government began to build highways. Soon, they connected distant parts of the United States.

Highways allowed people to travel great distances easily. They no longer had to rely only on trains. People could get in their cars and travel farther and faster than ever before.

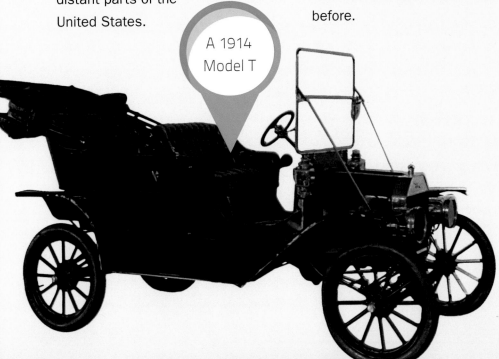

A 1914 Model T

The Television Transforms Entertainment

Television broadcasts the world into people's homes. But it started small in the 1920s. Scotsman John Logie Baird believed he could send images and sound using electricity. In 1926, he revealed the first working television. Its screen was just 3.5 inches (8.8 cm) by 2 inches (5 cm).

Regular television broadcasts began a few years later. Most television stations were in large cities, such as New York. Only people who lived nearby could get reception on their television. Broadcasts could not reach people who lived far away. Televisions were also expensive. For these reasons, the invention was slow to catch on.

Few television channels broadcast during World War II, from 1941 to 1945. After the war, there were only 6 television stations and 10,000 sets in the United States. Slowly, more stations started broadcasting. Even people who lived far from cities could now watch television. This inspired many people to buy their own sets. By 1950, more

By the late 1950s, many families had their own television sets.

than 100 stations were broadcasting shows. Americans owned 6 million sets.

Television quickly became a part of everyday life. It replaced reading, listening to the radio, and watching movies as the most popular form of entertainment. By the mid-1960s, American families watched as many as five hours of television each day.

Today, viewers no longer have to wait until a station broadcasts a show to watch it. They can watch programs on services that stream videos. Or, people can record a program for later on a DVR. New smart televisions also allow viewers to connect their televisions to the Internet.

116.4 million

Number of American homes with a television in 2014.

- The first successful television broadcasts happened in the 1920s.
- Television exploded in popularity after World War II.
- It changed the way people spent their time and were entertained.

A smart television allows viewers to surf the Internet, stream programs, and watch regular television broadcasts.

Antibiotics Save Lives

Antibiotics are life-saving medicines. Penicillin was the first antibiotic discovered. In 1928, scientist Alexander Fleming went away on vacation. When he returned, he found mold growing in a dish of bacteria in his lab. Fleming noticed that none of the bacteria grew near the mold. He realized that the mold kept the bacteria from growing. That mold was penicillin.

Researchers found that penicillin killed many types of bacteria. Soon, scientists at Oxford University were

Alexander Fleming studies bacteria in his lab in London, England.

experimenting with penicillin. They wanted to learn how to make and purify it.

In 1942, a Connecticut doctor first used penicillin successfully on a patient. The drug also saved many soldiers' lives during World War II. Doctors learned they could give patients penicillin to cure many different illnesses. This earned it the nickname "the wonder drug."

Since then, scientists have discovered other antibiotics. They help cure illnesses such as pneumonia, strep throat, and ear infections. The antibiotics kill the bacteria that cause them. Many of

200 million

Estimated number of lives that penicillin has saved.

- Alexander Fleming discovered penicillin, the first antibiotic, in 1928.
- In the early 1940s, Oxford scientists learned how to produce and purify large amounts of penicillin.
- With antibiotics, doctors can cure infections that were once deadly.

these illnesses were once deadly or had no treatment. Today, millions of people owe their lives to antibiotics.

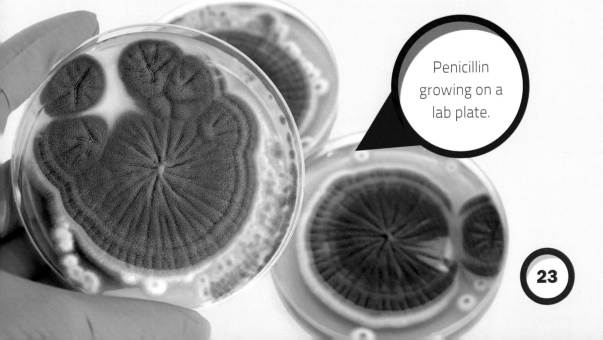

Penicillin growing on a lab plate.

The Internet Connects the World

The Internet brought a world of knowledge to humans' fingertips. In 1969, the US government created ARPANET. It was an early version of the Internet. It was designed for scientists to share research and data with each other. Only a few computers were connected.

In time, the Internet grew and changed. It became a broad network of computers. In 1991, the World Wide Web came into being. On it, people could create websites to share information. By 1993, more than 2 million computers were connected to the Internet.

Today, about three out of four American homes can connect to the Internet. Users can access a vast amount of information. Never before has knowledge been so easy to find.

People can express themselves in more ways, too. Writers can share opinions on blogs. Anyone can share comments on news articles, songs, products, or books.

The Internet also makes it easy for people to connect. E-mail allows people to send and receive messages instantly anywhere in the world. With social media, Internet users can create digital communities. No longer do people

THINK ABOUT IT

What other major inventions changed the way people communicate? How did they change it? Which do you think most changed communication? Why?

The Internet lets people learn, work, shop, bank, and get news at any time or in any place.

have to go to stores to shop. People can instantly order food, clothing, books, or other items online at any time of the day or night.

3 billion

Approximate number of people worldwide who can access the Internet.

- The US government created an early version of the Internet in 1969.
- In 1991, the World Wide Web was introduced.
- The Internet allowed people to shop, learn, socialize, and play in entirely new ways.

The Personal Computer Does It All

Personal computers (PCs) have become a major part of day-to-day life. Yet early computers were massive, often taking up an entire room. They were also costly and difficult to run. By the 1970s, new technology allowed computers to shrink in size and price. This led to personal computers.

Around 1977, computer companies began to sell PCs. From that point, computers

Personal computers are now common in schools, offices, and libraries.

took off. PCs were basic, but people could still type documents, make spreadsheets, and play games on them. A new technology called the microprocessor made computers smaller, faster, and more powerful. Starting in the 1990s, PCs also played a key role in connecting to the Internet.

Today, PCs are often found in offices, homes, and schools. In 2013, almost 85 percent of American homes had a personal computer. People depend on them for business, communication, and entertainment. They allow people to watch television shows, edit videos, send e-mail messages, and listen to music.

In 2015, nearly two-thirds of Americans owned smartphones.

288.7 million
Number of personal computers sold in 2015.

- Companies started selling personal computers in the 1970s.
- Personal computers are now common in offices, schools, and homes.
- People use personal computers daily for work and play.

POCKET POWER

Smartphones are pocket-sized personal computers. They may fit in a person's palm, but they hold advanced technology. Each year they become more and more powerful. Today's smartphones have even more power than all of NASA's computers did in 1969. That was the year NASA sent Apollo 11 to the moon.

Other Notable Inventions

Magnetic Compass

For centuries, sailors used the stars to guide their ships. On cloudy nights, this made sailing difficult. Around the 11th century, the Chinese realized that a magnetized needle always pointed south. They then invented the magnetic compass. Explorers were able to more safely and easily sail around the world.

Mechanical Refrigeration

Long ago, people stored food in cool streams or underground cellars to keep it from spoiling. In 1834, inventor Jacob Perkins created the first refrigerator. Refrigeration changed the way people ate. Perishable foods, such as meat and milk, could come from great distances. Refrigeration kept them from going bad on the journey.

Photography

French artist Louis-Jacques-Mandé Daguerre invented photography. In 1837, he discovered a combination of light and chemicals that created detailed pictures. These early photographs were called "daguerreotypes." Over the years, others improved the process. People were able to have portraits taken of themselves. They could also see pictures of distant lands and cultures.

The Atomic Bomb

During World War II, US scientists built an atomic bomb. They knew it would be much more powerful than regular bombs. In August 1945, the US military dropped two atomic bombs on Japan, its enemy. More than 120,000 Japanese died. The bombs ended the war. But people were shocked that the United States used such a powerful weapon on civilians. Since then, other nations have developed their own nuclear weapons.

Glossary

alchemist
A person who tried to discover immortality and change metals into gold.

aqueduct
A structure above ground that carries water from one place to another.

cast
A hard object that is made using a mold.

chamber pot
A container kept in a bedroom and used as a toilet.

filament
The part of a lightbulb that glows when electricity passes through.

immortality
The ability to live forever.

patent
To legally claim the right to an idea.

reservoir
A pool where water is stored.

suburb
An area at the edge of a city.

For More Information

Books

Bender, Lionel. *Invention*. New York: DK Publishing, 2013.

Spengler, Kremena. *An Illustrated Timeline of Inventions and Inventors*. Mankato, MN: Picture Window Books, 2012.

Turner, Tracey, Andrea Mills, and Clive Gifford. *100 Inventions That Made History: Brilliant Breakthroughs That Shaped Our World*. New York: DK Publishing, 2014.

Visit 12StoryLibrary.com

Scan the code or use your school's login at **12StoryLibrary.com** for recent updates about this topic and a full digital version of this book. Enjoy free access to:

- Digital ebook
- Breaking news updates
- Live content feeds
- Videos, interactive maps, and graphics
- Additional web resources

Note to educators: Visit 12StoryLibrary.com/register to sign up for free premium website access. Enjoy live content plus a full digital version of every 12-Story Library book you own for every student at your school.

Editor's note: The 12 topics featured in this book are selected by the author and approved by the book's editor. While not a definitive list, the selected topics are an attempt to balance the book's subject with the intended readership. To expand learning about this subject, please visit **12StoryLibrary.com** or use this book's QR code to access free additional content.

Index

About the Author

Emily Rose Oachs graduated from the University of Minnesota. She has authored more than 50 nonfiction books for children and young adults, on topics ranging from natural disasters and biomes to geography and history. She lives and writes in Los Angeles, California.

READ MORE FROM 12-STORY LIBRARY

Every 12-Story Library book is available in many formats. For more information, visit 12StoryLibrary.com.